Oxford
in Quotations

Bodleian Library
UNIVERSITY OF OXFORD

First published in 2014 by the
Bodleian Library
Broad Street
Oxford OX1 3BG
www.bodleianbookshop.co.uk

ISBN: 978 1 85124 400 3

Selection and arrangement © Bodleian Library
Cover design by Dot Little
Designed and typeset by Rod Teasdale in 11 on 13pt Jenson
Printed and bound by L.E.G.O. spa, Vicenza

British Library Catalogue in Publishing Data
A CIP record of this publication is available from
the British Library

> And that sweet City with her
> dreaming spires.

Matthew Arnold
(1822–1888)

"

I was a modest, good-humoured
boy. It is Oxford that has made
me insufferable.

Max Beerbohm
(1872–1956)

"

66

If I were not a King, I would be a University man; and if it were so that I must be a prisoner, if I might have my wish, I would desire to have no other prison than that [Bodleian] library, and to be chained together with so many good authors, *et mortuis magister*.

King James I
(1566–1625)

99

66

Oxford, the paradise of dead philosophies.

George Santayana
(1863–1952)

99

The clever men at Oxford,
Know all that there is to be knowed.
But they none of them know one half
    as much
As intelligent Mr. Toad!

Kenneth Grahame
(1859–1932)

"

[Oxford] is a sanctuary in which exploded systems and obsolete prejudices find shelter and protection after they have been hunted out of every corner of the world.

Adam Smith
(1723–1790)

"

In spite of the roaring of the young lions at the Union, and the screaming of the rabbits in the home of the vivisect, in spite of Keble College, and the tramways, and the sporting prints, Oxford still remains the most beautiful thing in England, and nowhere else are life and art so exquisitely blended, so perfectly made one.

Oscar Wilde
(1854–1900)

"

[Oxford] whispering from her towers the last enchantments of the Middle Age …

Home of lost causes, and forsaken beliefs, and unpopular names, and impossible loyalties!

Matthew Arnold
(1822–1888)

"

66

Oxford gave the world marmalade
and a manner, Cambridge science
and a sausage.

Anon.

99

"

There are few greater temptations
on earth than to stay permanently at
Oxford in meditation, and to read all
the books in the Bodleian.

Hilaire Belloc
(1870–1953)

"

66

You'd think they would advertise
this place to let people know it was
on the map.

A Chump At Oxford
1940

99

The King, observing with judicious eyes
    The state of both his universities,
To Oxford sent a troop of horse, and
    why?
That learned body wanted loyalty;
To Cambridge books, as very well
    discerning
How much that loyal body wanted
    learning.

Joseph Trapp
(1649–1747)

The King to Oxford sent a troop of
    horse,
For Tories own no argument but force:
With equal skill to Cambridge books he
    sent,
For Whigs admit no force but argument.

Sir William Browne
(1558–1610)

66

So poetry, which is in Oxford made
An art, in London only is a trade.

John Dryden
(1631–1700)

99

"

You will hear more good things
on the outside of a stagecoach from
London to Oxford than if you were
to pass a twelvemonth with the
undergraduates, or heads of colleges,
of that famous university.

William Hazlitt
(1778–1830)

"

"

If I had to do literary work of an absorbing character, Oxford is the last place in which I should attempt to do it.

Robert Cecil
(1830–1903)

"

66

I'm privileg'd to be very impertinent,
being an Oxonian.

George Farquhar
(1677–1707)

99

66

At Oxford, as you know, we follow the
Cambridge lead, sometimes with
uncertain steps.

Benjamin Jowett
(1817–1893)

99

I remember an acquaintance saying to me that 'the Oriel Common Room stank of logic'.

John Henry Newman
(1801–1890)

Undergraduates owe their happiness chiefly to the consciousness that they are no longer at school. The nonsense which was knocked out of them at school is all put gently back at Oxford or Cambridge.

Max Beerbohm
(1872–1956)

66

Oxford is low and subject to vapours.

Anthony Wood
(1632–1695)

99

66

I was therefore entered at Oxford and
have been properly idle ever since.

Jane Austen
(1775–1817)

99

"

At Oxford one was positively
encouraged to take wine during
tutorials. The tongue must be untied.

Christopher Hitchens
(1949–2011)

"

The two great turning points in my life,
were when my father sent me to Oxford,
and when society sent me to prison.

Oscar Wilde
(1854–1900)

Towery city and branchy between
    towers;
Cuckoo-echoing, bell-swarmèd, lark
    charmèd, rook-racked, river-rounded;
The dapple-eared lily below thee; that
    country and town did
Once encounter in, here coped & poisèd
    powers ...

Gerard Manley Hopkins
(1844–1889)

"

I often think how much easier the world would have been to manage if Herr Hitler and Signor Mussolini had been at Oxford.

Edward Wood, 1st Earl of Halifax (1881–1959)

"

What distinguishes Cambridge from Oxford, broadly speaking, is that nobody who has been to Cambridge feels compelled to write about it.

A.A. Milne
(1882–1956)

> It is dangerous sending a young man
> who is beautiful to Oxford.

Dudley Ryder
(1691–1756)

"

You spend your first term at Oxford
meeting interesting and exciting
people and the rest of your time there
avoiding them.

Evelyn Waugh
(1903–1966)

"

66

But Venice, like Oxford, had kept the background for romance, and, to the true romantic, background was everything, or almost everything.

Oscar Wilde
(1854–1900)

99

I would sooner send a young man to Rome than to Oxford. At the one he might be shocked and disgusted; but at the other he is cajoled, and cheated, and ruined.

Anthony Trollope
(1815–1882)

YE sacred Nurseries of blooming
   Youth!
In whose collegiate shelter England's
   Flowers
Expand – enjoying through their vernal
   hours
The air of liberty, the light of truth;
Much have ye suffered from Time's
   gnawing tooth,
Yet, O ye Spires of Oxford! Domes and
   Towers!
Gardens and Groves! your presence
   overpowers

The soberness of Reason; 'till, in sooth,
Transformed, and rushing on a bold
    exchange,
I slight my own beloved Cam, to range
Where silver Isis leads my stripling
    feet;
Pace the long avenue, or glide adown
The stream-like windings of that
    glorious street,
– An eager Novice robed in fluttering
    gown!

William Wordsworth
(1770–1850)

"

[The members of Queen's College] were all either stupid or dissipated. I learnt nothing. I played tennis once or twice ...

Jeremy Bentham
(1748–1832)

"

Anyone taking classics or history for the prestige is either at Oxford or stuck in 1909.

Laura Penny
(b. 1975)

66

Oxford is, and always has been, full of cliques, full of factions, and full of a particular non-social snobbiness.

Mary Warnock, Baroness Warnock (b. 1924)

99

The greatest gift that Oxford gives her sons is, I truly believe, a genial irreverence toward learning, and from that irreverence love may spring.

Robertson Davies
(1913–1995)

[Essential for success at Oxford:] plus fours; a repertoire of pornographic stories; some skill, legendary or otherwise, at golf; a Morris car; a sneer ... and an exhaustless capacity for suppurating self-conceit.

John George Sinclair
(1825–1912)

The truth is that Oxford is simply
a very beautiful city in which it is
convenient to segregate a certain
number of the young of the nation
while they are growing up.

Evelyn Waugh
(1903–1966)

Clad in beauty of dreams begotten
    Strange old city for ever young,
Keep the dreams that we have
    forgotten,
Keep the songs we have never sung.
So shall we hear your music calling,
So from a land where songs are few,
When the shadows of life are falling,
Mother, your sons come back to you.

Christ Church undergraduate
1915

66

Untruthful! My nephew Algernon?
Impossible! He is an Oxonian!

Oscar Wilde
(1854–1900)

99

'At least Oxford spies for us', as one portly academic once put it to me, 'while Cambridge seems to prefer to spy for the other side'.

Christopher Hitchens
(1949–2011)

> To call a man a characteristically Oxford man is, in my opinion, to give him the highest compliment that could be paid to any human being.

William Gladstone
(1809–1898)

"

A vision of greyroofed houses, a long
street and the sound of many bells ...

William Morris
(1834–1896)

"

"

The world surely has not another place
like Oxford; it is a despair to see such a
place and ever to leave it, for it would
take a lifetime and more than one to
comprehend and enjoy it satisfactorily.

Nathaniel Hawthorne
(1804–1864)

"

66

Upon beholding the masses of buildings at Oxford, devoted to what they call 'learning', I could not help reflecting on the drones that they contain and the wasps they send forth!

William Cobbett
(1763–1835)

99

"

... we could pass our lives at Oxford
without having or wanting any other
idea – that of the place is enough ...
Let him then who is fond of indulging
in dreamlike existence go to Oxford
and stay there.

William Hazlitt
(1778–1830)

"

"

Your masters at Oxford have taught you to idolize reason, drying up the prophetic capacities of your heart!

Umberto Eco
(b. 1932)

"

66

Going to Oxford didn't necessarily
make a person clever.

Arundhati Roy
(b. 1961)

99

" ... you can wander through a town like Oxford and in the space of a few hundred yards pass the home of Christopher Wren, the buildings where Halley found his comet and Boyle his first law, the track where Roger Bannister ran the first sub-four-minute mile, the meadow where Lewis Carroll strolled ...

Bill Bryson
(b. 1951)
"

"

Oxford is a little aristocracy in itself,
numerous and dignified enough to rank
with other estates in the realm.

Ralph Waldo Emerson
(1630–1720)

"

Oxford is so beautiful still that only those who know her history are sensible of any loss …

E. A. Greening Lamborn
(1877–1950)

... and their divided streams make several little sweet and pleasant islands, is seated on a rising vale the most famous University of Oxford, in Saxon Oxenford, our most noble Athens, the seat of the English Muses, the prop and pillar, nay the sun, the eye, the very soul of the nation; the most celebrated fountain of wisdom and learning, from whence Religion, Letters and Good Manners, are happily diffused thro' the whole Kingdom.

William Camden
(1551–1623)

He hath Oxford seen, for beauty,
    grace
And healthiness ne'er saw a better
    place.
If God himself on earth abode would
    make
The Oxford, sure, would for his
    dwelling take.

Daniel Rogers
(1538?–1591)

" The area by the Radcliffe Camera and the Bodleian is unique in the world, or if that seems a hazardous statement, it is certainly unparalleled at Cambridge.

Sir Nikolaus Pevsner
(1902–1983)

"

What a place to be in is an old library!
It seems as though all the souls of all
the writers, that have bequeathed their
labours to these Bodleians, were
reposing here, as in some dormitory, or
middle state ... I seem to inhale
learning, walking amid their foliage;
and the odour of their moth-scented
coverings is fragrant as the first bloom
of those sciential apples which grew
amid the happy orchard.

Charles Lamb
(1775–1834)

"

The high street is one of the world's
great streets. It has everything. It is
on a slight curve so that vistas ahead
always change.

Sir Nikolaus Pevsner
(1902–1983)

"

Like to a queen in pride of place, she
    wears
The splendour of a crown in Radcliffe's
    dome.

Lionel Johnson
(1867–1902)

66

Were it not for the important
colleges, the place would be not
unlike a large village.

Zacharias Conrad von Uffenbach
(1683–1734)

99

"

This Oxford, I have no doubt is the finest City in the world.

John Keats
(1795–1821)

"

66

Rome has been called the 'Sacred City':
might not our Oxford be called so too?

William Hazlitt
(1778–1830)

99

Oxford lends sweetness to labour and
dignity to leisure.

Henry James
(1843–1916)

Yet I have seen no place, by inland
   brook,
Hill-top or plain, or trim arcaded
   bowers,
That carries age so nobly in its look
As Oxford with the sun upon her
   towers.

F.W. Faber
(1814–1863)

"

In the summer term Oxford teaches
the exquisite art of idleness, one of
the most important things that any
University can teach, and possibly as
the first-fruits of the dreaming in grey
cloister and silant garden, which either
makes or mars a man …

Oscar Wilde
(1854–1900)

"

"

Noon strikes on England, noon on
    Oxford town,
Beauty she was statue cold – there's
    blood upon her gown.

James Elroy Flecker
(1884–1915)

"

"

I wonder anybody does anything at Oxford but dream and remember, the place is so beautiful. One almost expects the people to sing instead of speaking. It is all like an opera.

William Butler Yeats
(1865–1939)

"

66

At the present moment Oxford is the most dangerous place to which a young man can be sent.

Anthony Trollope
(1815–1882)

99

"

To the University of Oxford I
acknowledge no obligation; and she will
as cheerfully renounce me for a son, as I
am willing to disclaim her for a mother.
I spent fourteen months at Magdalen
College; they proved to be the fourteen
months the most idle and unprofitable
of my whole life.

Edward Gibbon
(1737–1794)

"

The Oxford manner is, alas, indefinable;
I was going to say indefensible.

Robert Baldwin Ross
(1869–1918)

66

A morning at Oxford without at least
three hours in the Bodleian Library
would be a crime.

Niall Ferguson
(b. 2013)

99

Oxford is on the whole more attractive than Cambridge to the ordinary visitor; and the traveller is therefore recommended to visit Cambridge first, or omit it altogether.

Karl Baedeker
(1801–1859)

"

Tea in Oxford ... is a manly affair ... [it] is another meal, and not the least of the day. And it ranks among the pleasantest of the day's occasions. Good tea gives a subtle eloquence to the tongue; and witty epigrams and noble schemes are born about the stroke of five in Oxford.

A Manual for Prospective Rhodes Scholars

1922

"

"

[...] it is a thing impossible to praise
in rhyme or prose the pleasures of tea
at Oxford.

Edward Thomas
(1878–1917)

"

The days of port and peace are gone
I am a modern Oxford don;
No more I haunt the candle's gloom,
The cosy chairs of Common-Room;
No more the senior man discourses
Of wine, of women fair, and horses …

Anon., *Oxford Magazine*
1894

66

Being published by the Oxford
University Press is rather like being
married to a duchess: the honour is
almost greater than the pleasure.

Rupert Hart-Davis
(1907–1999)

99

Bodley's Library seemed a perfect paradise for a student. I must confess that I slightly altered my opinion when I had to sit there every day during a severe winter without any fire, shivering and shaking and almost unable to hold my pen, till the kind Mr. Coxe, the sub-librarian, took compassion on me and brought me a splendid fur that had been sent him as a present by a Russian scholar, who had witnessed the misery of the librarian in this Siberian library.

Friedrich Max Müller
(1823–1900)

"

When going around these gloomy
chapels and halls it was necessary to say
to yourself about once every thirty
minutes 'This is a school. We are not
visiting a temple or an historic place but
we are seeing a school. This is a factory
where the future is brewed.'

Haruko Ichikawa
(1896–1943)

"

Gerard Langbaine's death in 1658 was [reported to have been] caused by 'extreme cold taken sitting in the University Library'.

Bodleian Staff Newsletter
1977

And I still have a definite notion
That Oxford must bear off the palm
For plain living, high thinking,
    devotion,
Enlightenment, culture and calm!

Anon., *Oxford Magazine*
1890

"

At Oxford he learned that the
importance of human beings has been
vastly overrated by specialists.

E.M. Forster
(1879–1970)

"

"

Oxford is Oxford: not a mere receptacle
for youth, like Cambridge. Perhaps it
wants its inmates to love it rather than
to love one another.

E.M. Forster
(1879–1970)

"

"

No sensible man who knows Oxford
would wish greatly to change it.

Samuel Eliot Morison
(1887–1976)

"

> Nobody outside Oxford knows, and nobody inside Oxford cares, if a certain professor be Communist or Fascist …

Samuel Eliot Morison
(1887–1976)

66

He degraded himself by the vice of
drinking, which, together with a great
stock of Greek and Latin, he brought
away with him from Oxford and
retained and practised ever afterwards.

Philip Dormer Stanhope
(1694–1773)

99

Oxford was their [nineteenth-century dons] world and beyond Oxford lay only wide wastes of shallowness and inaccuracy ...

J.R. Green
(1837–1883)

The dons of Oxford and Cambridge are too busy educating the young men to be able to teach them anything.

Samuel Butler
(1835–1902)

A self-made man is one who believes in luck and sends his son to Oxford.

Christina Stead
(1902–1983)

Credits

The publisher gratefully thanks the many copyright holders below who have generously granted permission for the use of the quotations in this book. Every effort has been made to credit copyright holders of the quotations used in this book. We apologize for any unintentional omissions or errors and will insert the appropriate acknowledgement to any companies or individuals in subsequent editions of the work.

p.1, Matthew Arnold, *Thyrsis* (1865); p.2, ©Estate of Max Beerbohm, *More* (1899); p.3, King James I, in Richard Burton, *Anatomy of Melancholy* (1621), pt.II, sc.2, mem.4; p.4, George Santayana, *Egotism in German Philosophy* (1915), p144; p.5, Kenneth Grahame, *The Wind in the Willows* (1908), ch.10; p.6, Adam Smith, *The Wealth of Nations* (1776), pt.III art.2; p.7, Oscar Wilde, Reviews (1908), *Dramatic Review*, 23 May, 1885; p.8, Matthew Arnold, *Thyrsis* (1865); p.10, Robert Speaight, *The Life of Hilaire Belloc* (1957), ch.5; p.12, Joseph Trapp, *Anecdotes* (1812–16), vol.3, p.330; p.13, William Browne, Reply to Trapp's epigram, in J. Nichols, *Literary Anecdotes* vol.3 (1812), p.330; p.14, John Dryden, 'Prologue and Epilogue to the University of Oxford' (1673); p.15, William Hazlitt, *Table Talk* vol.1 (1821), 'The Ignorance of the Learned'; p.16, Robert Cecil, Letter to William Sanday, 30 May 1900; p.17, George Farquhar, *Sir Harry Wildair*, Act II (1701); p.18, Benjamin Jowett, Letter to Professor Marshall, 5 Jan. 1886; p.19, John Henry Newman (1865), *History of My Religious Opinions from 1841 to 1845*, pt.6; p.20, Max Beerbohm, *More* (1922), p.170; p.21, Anthony Wood, *Survey of the antiquities of the city of Oxford*, vol.15, p.26; p.22, Jane Austen, *Sense and Sensibility*, ch.19; p.23, *Hitch-22* (2010), p.351, ©Estate of Christopher Hitchens, reprinted by permission of Atlantic Books Ltd; p.24, Oscar Wilde, *De Profundis* (1913); p.25, Gerard Manley Hopkins, *Dun's Scotus' Oxford*; p.26, ©Estate of Edward Wood, First Earl of Halifax, speech, 4 Nov. 1937, York; p.27, ©Estate of A.A. Milne, *It's Too Late Now*, (1939); p.28, Dudley Ryder, (1716), quoted in Arthur Marwick, *Beauty in History*, ch.4 (1988); p.29, ©Estate of Evelyn Waugh, *Brideshead Revisited* (1945), pt.1, ch.1; p30, Oscar Wilde, *The Picture of Dorian Gray* (1890), ch.14; p.31, Anthony Trollope, *Castle Richmond* (1860), ch.10; p.32 William Wordsworth, 'Oxford'; p.34, *The Works of Jeremy Bentham* (1842), p.42; p.35, ©Laura Penny, *More Money than Brains* (2010), ch.1; p.36, ©Mary Warnock, Baroness Warnock, *The Observer*, 2 Nov. 1980; p.37, ©Estate of Robertson Davies, *The Enthusiasms of Robertson Davies* (1979), p.293; p.38, J.G. Sinclair, *Portrait of Oxford* (1931), p.81; p.39, Evelyn Waugh, *Daily Mail*, 5 July 1930, p.8; p.41, Oscar Wilde, *The Importance of Being Earnest*, Act III; p.42, *Hitch-22* (2010), p.65, ©Estate of Christopher Hitchens, reprinted by permission of Atlantic Books Ltd, p.65; p.43, William Gladstone, Speech to Oxford Union, 1890; p.44, William Morris, *A Dream of John Ball*, ch.2; p.45, Nathaniel Hawthorne, *A Series of English Sketches* (1863), 'Near Oxford'; p.46, William Cobbett, *Rural Rides* (1830); p.47, William Hazlitt, 'Oxford', in *London Magazine*, 1823; p.48, ©Umberto Eco, *The Name of the Rose* (1995), p.63; p.49, ©Arundhati Roy, *The God of Small Things* (1997), p.56; p.50, ©Bill Bryson, *Notes from a Small Island* (1995), p.225; p51, Ralph Waldo Emerson, *Essays and English Traits*, ch.12; p.52. E.A. Greening Lamborn, in R. Tames, *A Traveller's History of Oxford* (2002), p.14; p.53, William Camden, *Britannia* (1586), 'Oxfordshire'; p.54, Daniel Rogers (1580), in *The Minstrelsy of*

Isis, ed. J.B. Firth (1908); p.55, Jennifer Sherwood and Nikolaus Pevsner, *Oxfordshire, The Buildings of England* (1974), p.254; p.56, Charles Lamb, 'Oxford in the Vacation', *Essays of Elia* (1823); p.57, Jennifer Sherwood and Nikolaus Pevsner, *Oxfordshire, The Buildings of England* (1974), p.307; p.58, *Some Poems of Lionel Johnson* (1922), p.32; p.59, Zacharias Conrad von Uffenbach, in John Doughill, *Oxford in English Literature* (1998), p.54; p.60 John Keats, Letter to Fanny Keats, Sept. 10, 1817; p.61 William Hazlitt, 'Oxford', *London Magazine*, 1823; p.62, Henry James, *Portraits of Places* (1883), 'English Vignettes', V; p.63, F.W. Faber, 'Aged Cities', *Poems* (1856); p.64, Oscar Wilde, Review of 'Primavera' in *Pall Mall Gazette*, 24 May 1890; p.65, James Elroy Flecker, 'The Dying Patriot' (1915); p.66, William Butler Yeats, Letter to Katharine Tynan, 25 Aug. 1888; p.67, Anthony Trollope, *Castle Richmond* (1860), ch.10; p.68, Edward Gibbon, *Memoirs of My Life* (1796), ch.3; p.69, Robert Baldwin Ross, *Masques and Phases, The Brand of Isis* (1909) ; p.70, ©Niall Ferguson, 'The Perfect Oxford Day'; p.71, Baedeker's *Great Britain* (1887), 'From London to Oxford'; p.73 Edward Thomas, *Oxford* (1903); p.75, G.M. Young, In Rupert-Hart Davies, Letter to George Lyttelton, 29 April 1956; p.76, Friedrich Max Müller, *My Autobiography, A Fragment* (1901), in Edmund Craster, *History of the Bodleian Library* (1845–1945), (1952); p.77, Haruko Ichikawa, *A Japanese Lady in England* (1937), p.192; pp.80, 81, ©Estate of E.M. Forster, *Howard's End* (1910), ch.12; pp.82, 83, ©Estate of Samuel Eliot Morison, 'An American Professor's Reflections on Oxford', *London Spectator* (7 Nov., 1925); p.84, Philip Dormer Stanhope, *Miscellaneous Works*, 'Lord Granville'; p.85, J.R. Green, in *St. Petersburg Times*, 9 July 1983, p.15; p.86, Samuel Butler, *Notebooks*; p.87, ©Estate of Christina Stead, *House of All Nations* (1938), 'Credo'.